North Dakota Ecoregions

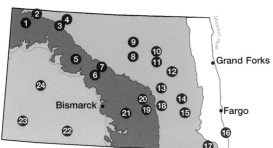

- ☐ Northwestern Great Plains
- ☐ Northern Glaciated Plains
- ☐ Northwestern Glaciated Plains
- ☐ Lake Agassiz Plain

Grand Forks
Bismarck
Fargo

1. Lake Zahl National Wildlife Refuge
2. Crosby Wetland Management District
3. Lostwood National Wildlife Refuge
4. Des Lacs National Wildlife Refuge
5. Hiddenwood National Wildlife Refuge
6. Audubon National Wildlife Refuge
7. Lake Nettie National Wildlife Refuge
8. Buffalo Lake National Wildlife Refuge
9. Pleasant Lake National Wildlife Refuge
10. Devils Lake Wetland Management District
11. Sullys Hill National Game Preserve
12. Johnson Lake National Wildlife Refuge
13. Arrowwood National Wildlife Refuge
14. Tomahawk National Wildlife Refuge
15. Stoney Slough National Wildlife Refuge
16. Rodger Ehnstrom Nature Center at Chahinkapa Zoo
17. Tewaukon National Wildlife Refuge
18. Frontier Village & National Buffalo Museum
19. Half-Way Lake National Wildlife Refuge
20. Chase Lake National Wildlife Refuge
21. Long Lake National Wildlife Refuge
22. Pretty Rock National Wildlife Refuge
23. Stewart Lake National Wildlife Refuge
24. Lake Ilo National Wildlife Refuge

NORTH DAKOTA WILDLIFE

A Folding Pocket Guide to Familiar Animals

(spine) NORTH DAKOTA WILDLIFE – A Folding Pocket Guide to Familiar Animals

A POCKET NATURALIST® GUIDE

WATERFORD PRESS

Green Darner
Anax junius
To 3 in. (8 cm)
Has a bright green thorax and a blue body. Like most dragonflies, it rests with its wings open.

Familiar Bluet
Enallagma civile
1.5 in. (4 cm)
Like most damselflies, it rests with its wings closed.

Field Cricket
Gryllus pennsylvanicus
To 1 in. (3 cm)
Song is a series of three chirps.

Twelve-spotted Skimmer
Libellula pulchella
To 2 in. (5 cm)
Each wing features black patches at the base, midpoint and tip.

Dog Day Cicada
Tibicen chloromera
To 1.5 in. (4 cm)
Song is a sudden loud whine or buzz, maintained steadily before dying away.

Convergent Lady Beetle
Hippodamia convergens
To .5 in. (1.3 cm)
North Dakota's state insect.

Water Boatman
Family Corixidae
To .5 in. (1.3 cm)
Swims erratically.

Water Strider
Gerris remigis
To .5 in. (1.3 cm)
'Skates' on the surface of quiet waters.

Honey Bee
Apis mellifera
To .75 in. (2 cm)
Slender bee has pollen baskets on its rear legs. Can only sting once.

Wasp
Vespula spp.
To .63 in. (1.6 cm)
Aggressive picnic pest can sting repeatedly.

Bumble Bee
Bombus spp.
To 1 in. (3 cm)
Stout, furry bee is large and noisy. Can sting repeatedly.

Paper Wasp
Polistes spp.
To 1 in. (3 cm)
Told by slender profile and dark, pale-banded abdomen. Builds papery hanging nests. Can sting repeatedly.

Western Black Widow
Latrodectus hesperus
To .5 in. (1.3 cm)
Has red hourglass marking on abdomen. Venomous.

Goldenrod Crab Spider
Misumena vatia
To .4 in. (1 cm)

Black-and-yellow Garden Spider
Argiope aurantia
To 1.25 in. (3.2 cm)

Canadian Tiger Swallowtail
Papilio canadensis
To 3 in. (8 cm)
A smaller version of the eastern tiger swallowtail.

Black Swallowtail
Papilio polyxenes
To 3.5 in. (9 cm)

Common Sulphur
Colias philodice
To 2 in. (5 cm)
Common in open areas and along roadsides.

Common Checkered Skipper
Pyrgus communis
To 1.25 in. (3.2 cm)

Viceroy
Limenitis archippus
To 3 in. (8 cm)
Told from similar monarch by its smaller size and the thin, black band on its hindwings.

Cabbage White
Pieris rapae
To 2 in. (5 cm)
One of the most common butterflies.

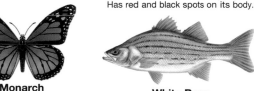

Red Admiral
Vanessa atalanta
To 2.5 in. (6 cm)

Painted Lady
Vanessa cardui
To 2.5 in. (6 cm)
Tip of forewing is dark with white spots.

Monarch
Danaus plexippus
To 4 in. (10 cm)

Mourning Cloak
Nymphalis antiopa
To 3.5 in. (9 cm)
Emerges during the first spring thaw.

Common Wood-Nymph
Cercyonis pegala
To 3 in. (8 cm)
Note 2 'eyespots' on the forewing.

Great Spangled Fritillary
Speyeria cybele
To 3 in. (8 cm)
Common in marshes and wet meadows.

Eastern Tailed Blue
Everes comyntas
To 1 in. (3 cm)
Note orange spots above thread-like hindwing tails.

White Admiral
Limenitis arthemis arthemis
To 3 in. (8 cm)
Common in upland deciduous forests.

Comma
Polygonia comma
To 3 in. (8 cm)
Has a silvery comma mark on the underside of its hindwings.

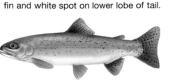

Sauger
Sander canadensis To 30 in. (75 cm)
Note dark 'saddles' on back.

Walleye
Sander vitreus To 40 in. (1 m)
Note dark blotch on rear of first dorsal fin and white spot on lower lobe of tail.

Chinook (King) Salmon
Oncorhynchus tshawytscha
To 5 ft. (1.5 m)
Has dark spots on back and tail.

Rainbow Trout
Oncorhynchus mykiss To 44 in. (1.1 m)
Note reddish side stripe.

Brown Trout
Salmo trutta To 40 in. (1 m)
Has red and black spots on its body.

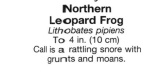

White Bass
Morone chrysops To 18 in. (45 cm)
Silvery fish has 4-7 dark side stripes.

Bluegill
Lepomis macrochirus To 16 in. (40 cm)

Largemouth Bass
Micropterus salmoides To 40 in. (1 m)
Note prominent side spots. Jaw joint extends past eye.

Crappie
Pomoxis spp. To 16 in. (40 cm)

Smallmouth Bass
Micropterus dolomieu To 27 in. (68 cm)
Jaw joint is beneath the eye.

Yellow Perch
Perca flavescens To 16 in. (40 cm)
Note 6-9 dark 'saddles' down its side.

Northern Pike
Esox lucius To 53 in. (1.4 m)
North Dakota's state fish.

Channel Catfish
Ictalurus punctatus To 4 ft. (1.2 m)

Muskellunge
Esox masquinongy
To 6 ft. (1.8 m)
Has dark, vertical side bars. Prized sport fish is an aggressive predator.

Wood Frog
Lithobates sylvaticus
To 3 in. (8 cm)
Note dark mask. Staccato call is duck-like.

Great Plains Toad
Anaxyrus cognatus
To 4 in. (10 cm)
Call is a metallic trill.

Dakota Toad
Bufo hemiophrys
To 3 in. (8 cm)

Northern Leopard Frog
Lithobates pipiens
To 4 in. (10 cm)
Call is a rattling snore with grunts and moans.

Plains Spadefoot Toad
Scaphiopus bombifrons
To 2.5 in. (6 cm)
Note vertical pupils.

Chorus Frog
Pseudacris triseriata
To 1.5 in. (4 cm)
Call sounds like a thumbnail running over the teeth of a comb.

Tiger Salamander
Ambystoma mavortium
To 13 in. (33 cm)

Western Painted Turtle
Chrysemys picta bellii
To 10 in. (25 cm)

Snapping Turtle
Chelydra serpentina
To 18 in. (45 cm)
Note long tail.

Red-sided Garter Snake
Thamnophis sirtalis parietalis
To 4 ft. (1.2 m)

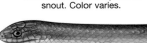

Western Hognose Snake
Heterodon nasicus To 3 ft. (90 cm)
Thick snake has an upturned snout. Color varies.

Plains Garter Snake
Thamnophis radix To 40 in. (1 m)

Yellow-bellied Racer
Coluber constrictor
To 6 ft. (1.8 m)

Gopher Snake
Pituophis catenifer To 8 ft. (2.4 m)
Note pointed snout.

Prairie Rattlesnake
Crotalus viridis
To 5 ft. (1.5 m)
Venomous snake is found in western ND.

Smooth Green Snake
Opheodrys vernalis To 26 in. (65 cm)

Canada Goose
Branta canadensis
To 45 in. (1.14 m)

Snow Goose
Chen caerulescens
To 31 in. (78 cm)

Greater White-fronted Goose
Anser albifrons
To 30 in. (75 cm)
Note white white ring at bill base.

Tundra Swan
Cygnus columbianus
To 4.5 ft. (1.4 m)
Note yellow mark on black bill.

Western Grebe
Aechmophorus occidentalis
To 25 in. (63 cm)

Mallard
Anas platyrhynchos To 28 in. (70 cm)

Blue-winged Teal
Spatula discors To 16 in. (40 cm)

Redhead
Aythya americana To 22 in. (55 cm)

Canvasback
Aythya valisineria To 2 ft. (60 cm)
Note sloping forehead and black bill.

Northern Pintail
Anas acuta To 30 in. (75 cm)

Wood Duck
Aix sponsa To 20 in. (50 cm)

American Coot
Fulica americana To 16 in. (40 cm)

Common Merganser
Mergus merganser To 27 in. (68 cm)

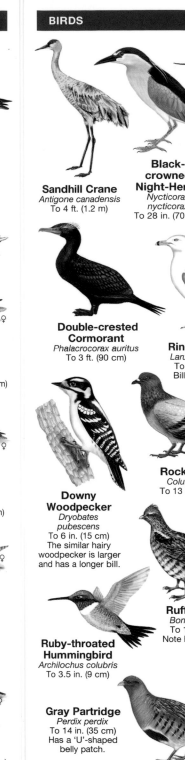

Sandhill Crane
Antigone canadensis
To 4 ft. (1.2 m)

Black-crowned Night-Heron
Nycticorax nycticorax
To 28 in. (70 cm)

American Avocet
Recurvirostra americana
To 20 in. (50 cm)

Great Blue Heron
Ardea herodias
To 4.5 ft. (1.4 m)

Double-crested Cormorant
Phalacrocorax auritus
To 3 ft. (90 cm)

Ring-billed Gull
Larus delawarensis
To 20 in. (50 cm)
Bill has dark ring.

American White Pelican
Pelecanus erythrorhynchos
To 5 ft. (1.5 m)

Downy Woodpecker
Dryobates pubescens
To 6 in. (15 cm)
The similar hairy woodpecker is larger and has a longer bill.

Rock Pigeon
Columba livia
To 13 in. (33 cm)

Mourning Dove
Zenaida macroura
To 13 in. (33 cm)
Call is a mournful – ooah-woo-woo-woo.

Ruffed Grouse
Bonasa umbellus
To 19 in. (48 cm)
Note black tail band.

Sharp-tailed Grouse
Tympanuchus phasianellus
To 20 in. (50 cm)
Tail is short and pointed.

Ruby-throated Hummingbird
Archilochus colubris
To 3.5 in. (9 cm)

Gray Partridge
Perdix perdix
To 14 in. (35 cm)
Has a 'U'-shaped belly patch.

Ring-necked Pheasant
Phasianus colchicus
To 3 ft. (90 cm)

Northern Harrier
Circus hudsonius
To 22 in. (55 cm)
Note white rump.

Red-tailed Hawk
Buteo jamaicensis
To 25 in. (63 cm)

Bald Eagle
Haliaeetus leucocephalus
To 40 in. (1 m)

Golden Eagle
Aquila chrysaetos
To 40 in. (1 m)

Great Horned Owl
Bubo virginianus
To 25 in. (63 cm)
Call is a resonant – hoo-HOO-hoooo.

Horned Lark
Eremophila alpestris
To 8 in. (20 cm)

House Wren
Troglodytes aedon
To 5 in. (13 cm)

Tree Swallow
Tachycineta bicolor
To 6 in. (15 cm)

White-breasted Nuthatch
Sitta carolinensis
To 6 in. (15 cm)

Eastern Bluebird
Sialia sialis
To 7 in. (18 cm)

Black-capped Chickadee
Poecile atricapillus
To 6 in. (15 cm)
Name-saying call is – chick-a-dee-dee-dee.

Barn Swallow
Hirundo rustica
To 8 in. (20 cm)
Note deeply forked tail.

Red-winged Blackbird
Agelaius phoeniceus
To 9 in. (23 cm)

American Robin
Turdus migratorius
To 11 in. (28 cm)

Yellow-headed Blackbird
Xanthocephalus xanthocephalus
To 11 in. (28 cm)

American Crow
Corvus brachyrhynchos
To 22 in. (55 cm)

Common Grackle
Quiscalus quiscula
To 14 in. (35 cm)

European Starling
Sturnus vulgaris
To 8 in. (20 cm)

Brown-headed Cowbird
Molothrus ater
To 7 in. (18 cm)

Black-billed Magpie
Pica hudsonia
To 22 in. (55 cm)

Blue Jay
Cyanocitta cristata
To 14 in. (35 cm)

Baltimore Oriole
Icterus galbula
To 8 in. (20 cm)

Western Meadowlark
Sturnella neglecta
To 9 in. (23 cm)
North Dakota's state bird.

Cedar Waxwing
Bombycilla cedrorum
To 7 in. (18 cm)
Red wing marks look like waxy droplets.

Spotted Towhee
Pipilo maculatus
To 9 in. (23 cm)

Dark-eyed Junco
Junco hyemalis
To 7 in. (18 cm)

Snow Bunting
Plectrophenax nivalis
To 8 in. (20 cm)

House Sparrow
Passer domesticus
To 6 in. (15 cm)

American Goldfinch
Spinus tristis
To 5 in. (13 cm)

House Finch
Haemorhous mexicanus
To 6 in. (15 cm)

Big Brown Bat
Eptesicus fuscus
To 5 in. (13 cm)

Eastern Gray Squirrel
Sciurus carolinensis
To 20 in. (50 cm)

Deer Mouse
Peromyscus maniculatus
To 8 in. (20 cm)
Distinguished by its white undersides and hairy tail.

Fox Squirrel
Sciurus niger
To 28 in. (70 cm)
Note large size and bushy tail.

House Mouse
Mus musculus
To 8 in. (20 cm)
Introduced pest has a naked tail.

Thirteen-lined Ground Squirrel
Spermophilus tridecemlineatus
To 12 in. (30 cm)

Norway Rat
Rattus norvegicus
To 18 in. (45 cm)
Brown to gray rodent has a naked tail.

Eastern Cottontail
Sylvilagus floridanus
To 18 in. (45 cm)

Black-tailed Prairie Dog
Cynomys ludovicianus
To 16 in. (40 cm)

Common Porcupine
Erethizon dorsatum
To 3 ft. (90 cm)
Large rodent has barbed quills near its rear that it uses for defense.

White-tailed Jackrabbit
Lepus townsendii
To 26 in. (65 cm)
Note large ears and white tail.

Long-tailed Weasel
Mustela frenata
To 21 in. (53 cm)

American Beaver
Castor canadensis
To 4 ft. (1.2 m)

Mink
Neovison vison
To 28 in. (70 cm)
Chin is white.

Common Raccoon
Procyon lotor
To 40 in. (1 m)

Common Muskrat
Ondatra zibethicus
To 2 ft. (60 cm)
Aquatic rodent has a naked tail that is flattened on its sides.

American Badger
Taxidea taxus
To 35 in. (88 cm)

Northern River Otter
Lontra canadensis
To 52 in. (1.3 m)

Striped Skunk
Mephitis mephitis
To 32 in. (80 cm)

Red Fox
Vulpes vulpes
To 40 in. (1 m)

Coyote
Canis latrans
To 52 in. (1.3 m)

White-tailed Deer
Odocoileus virginianus
To 7 ft. (2.1 m)

Bobcat
Lynx rufus
To 4 ft. (1.2 m)

American Bison
Bos bison To 12 ft. (3.6 m)

Pronghorn
Antilocapra americana
To 5 ft. (1.5 m)
Note 'pronged' horns.